MOCKTAIL MAGIC

101 WAYS TO SIP, SHARE, AND CELEBRATE

PUBLISHED BY BONDJOUR

ISBN: 9798883873590

WHO'S READY TO PARTY?

At Bondjour, we are all about fostering connections. Part of that is ensuring that everyone feels comfortable and welcome when you host an event and for this reason, many people like to offer an alcohol-free option.

Our book of mocktails ensures that whatever beverage choice your guests may make, they don't have to miss out on flavor or experience. From tangy citrus drinks to tropical mixes that transport you to the islands, this collection has something for everyone.

Each recipe is designed to serve two and can be scaled up accordingly for groups.

So grab your cocktail shaker and get sipping!

Cheers!
Team Bondjour

TABLE OF CONTENTS

TABLE OF CONTENTS

TABLE OF CONTENTS

TABLE OF CONTENTS

TABLE OF CONTENTS

TABLE OF CONTENTS

TABLE OF CONTENTS

TABLE OF CONTENTS

CITRUS
CELEBRATIONS

CITRUS BLISS

A refreshing morning pick-me-up, perfect for a sunny brunch or as a revitalizing afternoon beverage.

INGREDIENTS

1 cup orange juice
1/2 cup grapefruit juice
2 tablespoons honey
Sparkling water
Orange slices for garnish

1 In a shaker, combine orange juice, grapefruit juice, and honey. Shake well, until the honey is fully dissolved.

2 Pour the mixture into glasses filled with ice. Top with sparkling water.

3 Garnish with orange slices. Enjoy immediately!

MINTY CITRUS COOLER

A cooling and invigorating mocktail, perfect for a warm afternoon or as a palate cleanser between courses.

INGREDIENTS

1 cup limeade
1/2 cup orange juice
2 tablespoons mint simple syrup*
Club soda
Mint sprigs for garnish

*page 119

1 Mix limeade, orange juice, and mint syrup in a shaker. Shake well to infuse mint flavor.

2 Strain into glasses over ice. Top with club soda for a refreshing effervescence.

3 Garnish with mint. Enjoy immediately!

ZESTY LEMONADE FIZZ

A light and effervescent drink, perfect for a warm summer day or a casual outdoor gathering.

INGREDIENTS

1 cup fresh lemonade
1/2 cup lime juice
2 tablespoons agave syrup
Club soda
Fresh mint leaves for garnish

1 Mix fresh lemonade, lime juice, and agave syrup in a pitcher. Stir until well combined.

2 Top with club soda. Pour into ice-filled glasses.

3 Garnish with fresh mint leaves.

TANGY TANGERINE SPARKLE

A tropical-inspired mocktail, perfect for a weekend escape or to transport yourself to a sun-soaked paradise.

INGREDIENTS

1 cup tangerine juice
1/2 cup pineapple juice
2 tablespoons maple syrup
Ginger ale
Tangerine slices for garnish

1 Combine tangerine juice, pineapple juice, and maple syrup in a mixing glass. Stir until maple syrup is fully integrated.

2 Pour into glasses over ice. Top with ginger ale for a delightful sparkle.

3 Garnish with tangerine slices. Enjoy immediately!

CITRUS MINT FUSION

Perfect for a lively summer afternoon or casual outdoor gathering. Whether at a poolside barbecue or brunch, this mocktail offers a revitalizing experience, making it ideal for socializing and relaxation.

INGREDIENTS

I cup orange juice
1/2 cup grapefruit juice
Fresh mint leaves
Soda water

1 Mix orange and grapefruit juice, muddle mint leaves, and shake with ice.

2 Strain into glasses and top with soda water.

3 Serve immediately and enjoy!

LAVENDER LEMON DREAM

A soothing blend of lavender and zesty lemon, it is a perfect mocktail for serene moments. Ideal for lazy afternoons or cozy evenings, it offers a refreshing and peaceful escape with every sip.

INGREDIENTS
1/4 cup lavender-
infused water*
I Lemonade
I tablespoon agave
syrup
Edible flowers for
garnish
Crushed ice

*page 120

1 Combine lavender-infused water with lemonade with agave syrup.

2 Shake with ice and strain over crushed ice.

3 Garnish with edible flowers. Serve and enjoy!

GRAPEFRUIT ROSEMARY REFRESHER

A sophisticated mocktail with herbal notes, ideal for a dinner party or an evening of relaxation.

INGREDIENTS

1 cup fresh grapefruit juice
1/2 cup cranberry juice
2 tablespoons rosemary simple syrup*
Soda water
Rosemary sprigs for garnish

*page 119

1 Mix grapefruit juice, cranberry juice, and rosemary simple syrup in a cocktail shaker. Shake well to infuse flavors.

2 Strain into glasses over ice. Top with soda water for a fizzy twist.

3 Garnish with rosemary sprigs. Enjoy immediately!

CITRUS BASIL BREEZE

A light and herbaceous mocktail, perfect for a garden party or a springtime gathering.

INGREDIENTS

1 cup orange juice
1/2 cup lemonade
2 tablespoons agave nectar
Sparkling water
Fresh basil leaves for garnish

1 Combine orange juice, lemonade, and agave nectar in a pitcher. Stir until agave nectar is fully dissolved.

2 Top with sparkling water for a bubbly twist.

3 Pour into glasses filled with ice. Garnish with fresh basil leaves.

PINEAPPLE CITRUS FUSION

A tropical-inspired mocktail, perfect for a beach picnic or a summer gathering with friends.

INGREDIENTS

1 cup pineapple juice
1/2 cup orange juice
2 tablespoons coconut water
Sparkling water
Pineapple wedges for garnish

1 Mix pineapple juice, orange juice, and coconut water in a pitcher. Stir until well combined.

2 Pour into glasses filled with ice. Top with sparkling water for a tropical fizz.

3 Garnish with pineapple wedges. Serve immediately!

CITRUS GINGER ZING

A lively and invigorating mocktail, perfect for a midday energy boost or as a unique alternative to traditional sodas.

INGREDIENTS

1 cup grapefruit juice
1/2 cup lemon-lime soda
2 tablespoons ginger simple syrup*
Ice cubes
Thin slices of ginger for garnish

*page 119

1 Combine grapefruit juice, lemon-lime soda, and ginger simple syrup in a mixing glass.
Stir until well blended.

2 Pour over ice in glasses.

3 Garnish with thin slices of ginger for an extra kick.

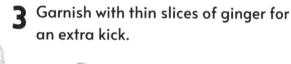

CITRUS LAVENDER LULLABY

Perfect for unwinding after a long day or a quiet evening, the Citrus Lavender Lullaby combines the vibrant citrus flavors with the calming aroma of lavender, creating a soothing and refreshing mocktail experience.

INGREDIENTS

I cup mixed citrus juice (orange, grapefruit, lemon)
1/4 teaspoon dried lavender buds
I tablespoon agave syrup
I cup lavender-infused water*
Citrus slices for garnish
Ice cubes

*page 120

1 In a shaker, combine mixed citrus juice, dried lavender buds, and agave syrup. Shake well to infuse the flavors, then strain into two glasses filled with ice.

2 Top up with lavender-infused water for a soothing touch. Stir gently to create the Citrus Lavender Lullaby blend.

3 Garnish with citrus slices for a visually appealing presentation.

RASPBERRY LEMONADE BREEZE

Perfect for a picnic or a sunny day at the park, the Raspberry Lemonade Breeze offers a burst of refreshing flavors with the combination of tart raspberries and citrusy lemon.

INGREDIENTS

1/2 cup raspberry puree
I tablespoon lemon juice
I tablespoon agave syrup
I cup lemon-lime flavored sparkling water
Fresh raspberries for garnish
Ice cubes

1 In a shaker, mix raspberry puree, lemon juice, and agave syrup.

2 Strain into two glasses filled with ice. Top up with lemon-lime flavored sparkling water. Stir gently.

3 Garnish with fresh raspberries. Enjoy the zesty and fruity Raspberry Lemonade Breeze.

BERRY CITRUS FUSION FIZZ

A vibrant and fruity mocktail, perfect for a festive occasion or to add a burst of flavor to a weekend celebration.

INGREDIENTS

I cup mixed berry juice (blueberry, raspberry, strawberry)
1/2 cup orange juice
2 tablespoons agave syrup
Sparkling water
Mixed berries for garnish

1 Combine mixed berry juice, orange juice, and agave syrup in a shaker. Shake well until agave syrup is fully dissolved.

2 Pour into glasses filled with ice. Top with sparkling water for a bubbly twist.

3 Garnish with mixed berries. Enjoy immediately!

CITRUS MINT MOJITO MOCKTAIL

A refreshing and herbaceous mocktail,
perfect for a lively gathering or to unwind
after a busy day.

INGREDIENTS

I cup limeade
2 tablespoons mint
leaves (muddled)
Soda water
Lime slices for garnish

1 Muddle mint leaves in the bottom of
a glass. Add limeade to the glass.

2 Stir well to incorporate mint flavor.
Fill the glass with ice and top with
soda water.

3 Garnish with lime slices.
Enjoy your refreshing mocktail
immediately!

LEMON LAVENDER DELIGHT

A fragrant and calming mocktail, perfect for a relaxing evening or to accompany a quiet moment of reflection.

INGREDIENTS

1 cup fresh lemonade
1/2 cup lavender-infused water*
2 tablespoons honey
Club soda
Lemon twists for garnish

*page 120

1 Mix fresh lemonade, lavender-infused water, and honey in a shaker. Shake well to combine flavors.

2 Strain into glasses over ice. Top with club soda for a light effervescence.

3 Garnish with lemon twists. Enjoy immediately!

STRAWBERRY BASIL LEMONADE

Perfect for a sunny day or a casual picnic, Strawberry Basil Lemonade offers a harmonious blend of sweet strawberries, aromatic basil, and zesty lemon, creating a refreshing and satisfying beverage.

INGREDIENTS

I cup fresh strawberries, hulled and halved
1/4 cup fresh basil leaves
Sparkling lemonade
Strawberry slices and basil sprigs for garnish
Ice cubes

1 In a blender, combine fresh strawberries, basil leaves, and sugar. Blend until smooth to create a vibrant strawberry-basil puree.

2 In a pitcher, mix the puree with sparkling lemonade to create the Strawberry Basil Lemonade. Pour the lemonade into glasses filled with ice.

3 Garnish with strawberry slices and basil sprigs for a fresh presentation.

CITRUS SUNRISE SPLASH

Perfect for a sunny afternoon, this vibrant drink mirrors the warmth of the season, providing a refreshing escape from the day.

INGREDIENTS

1 cup orange juice
1/2 cup pineapple juice
1 tablespoon grenadine
Ice cubes

1 Pour orange juice into glasses filled with ice. Slowly add pineapple juice, letting it settle.

2 Gently pour grenadine over the back of a spoon for a layered effect.

3 Stir before sipping for a burst of citrusy freshness.

ORANGE BASIL SANGRIA SPARKLE

A sophisticated and bubbly mocktail, perfect for a brunch gathering or to elevate your evening with a non-alcoholic alternative.

INGREDIENTS

I cup white grape juice
1/2 cup orange juice
2 tablespoons basil simple syrup*
Sparkling water
Orange and basil leaves for garnish

*page 119

1 Mix white grape juice, orange juice, and basil syrup in a pitcher.
Stir until well combined.

2 Pour into glasses over ice.
Top with sparkling water for a sangria-inspired sparkle.

3 Garnish with orange slices and basil leaves.
Enjoy immediately!

ORANGE BLISS FIZZ

Perfect for a sunny afternoon, Citrus Bliss Fizz provides a revitalizing blend of vitamin C and hydration, making it an ideal choice for a midday pick-me-up.

INGREDIENTS

I cup orange juice
Sparkling water
I tablespoon honey
Ice cubes
Orange slices for garnish

1 Start by combining orange juice, honey, and ice in a shaker. Shake well until the honey is dissolved.

2 Strain the mixture into two glasses filled with ice. Top up with sparkling water. Stir gently.

3 Garnish with orange slices. Enjoy this refreshing mocktail with a burst of citrus flavors.

HIBISCUS CITRUS ZING

Perfect for a lively seasonal gathering, the Hibiscus Citrus Zing infuses the floral essence of hibiscus with the refreshing zing of citrus, creating a vibrant and flavorful mocktail experience.

INGREDIENTS

1/2 cup cooled hibiscus tea
1/2 teaspoon freshly grated ginger
1 tablespoon honey
1/4 cup freshly squeezed orange juice
Sparkling water
Ice cubes
Orange slices for garnish

1 In a shaker, combine cooled hibiscus tea, freshly grated ginger, honey, and freshly squeezed orange juice. Shake well to blend the flavors, then strain into a glass filled with ice.

2 Top up with sparkling water for a zesty effervescence. Stir gently, ensuring the Hibiscus Citrus Zing is well-mixed. Garnish with orange slices for a citrusy visual appeal.

3 Sip and relish this delightful seasonal cocktail.

CITRUS MINTADE FUSION

A sweet and refreshing mocktail, perfect for a casual afternoon with friends or as a delightful accompaniment to a light meal.

INGREDIENTS

1 cup lemonade
1/2 cup orange juice
Mint leaves
1 tablespoon honey
Soda water
Mint leaves for garnish

1 Muddle orange juice, mint leaves, and honey in a shaker. Add the lemonade and shake well to blend flavors.

2 Strain into glasses over ice. Top with soda water for a fizzy kick.

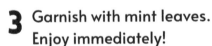

3 Garnish with mint leaves. Enjoy immediately!

CITRUS CUCUMBER COOLER

A hydrating and revitalizing mocktail, perfect for a post-workout refreshment or to cool down on a hot day.

INGREDIENTS

1 cup cucumber juice
1/2 cup orange juice
2 tablespoons agave syrup
Club soda
Cucumber slices for garnish

1 Mix cucumber juice, orange juice, and agave syrup in a pitcher. Stir until agave syrup is fully dissolved.

2 Pour into glasses filled with ice. Top with club soda for a crisp finish.

3 Garnish with cucumber slices. Enjoy immediately!

CITRUS BASIL MARTINI MOCKTAIL

A classy and alcohol-free alternative to a traditional martini, perfect for a cocktail party or a refined evening with friends.

INGREDIENTS

1 cup orange juice
1/2 cup lemonade
2 tablespoons basil simple syrup*
Sparkling water
Lemon twists for garnish

*page 119

1 Mix orange juice, lemonade, and basil syrup in a shaker. Shake well to infuse basil flavor.

2 Strain into martini glasses. Top with sparkling water for a sophisticated touch.

3 Garnish with lemon twists. Enjoy immediately!

FRUITY FUN

BERRY BLISS FIZZ

Perfect for a sunny afternoon picnic, the Berry Bliss Fizz offers a refreshing and sweet kick, making it an ideal companion to enjoy the great outdoors.

INGREDIENTS

I cup mixed berries (strawberries, blueberries, raspberries)
1/2 cup sparkling water
2 tablespoons honey
Ice cubes

1 Start by muddling the mixed berries in a shaker. Add honey and shake well.

2 Strain the mixture into glasses filled with ice, and top it off with sparkling water.

3 Garnish with a berry skewer for a burst of flavor in every sip. Enjoy immediately!

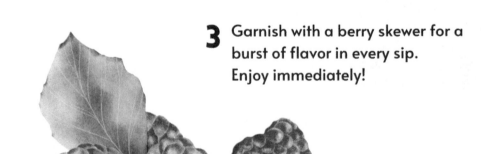

MYSTICAL BERRY ELIXIR

Unwind after a long day with the Mystical Berry Elixir, a soothing mocktail that transports you to a world of relaxation, making it an excellent choice for an evening wind-down.

INGREDIENTS

1 cup blackberries
1 cup pomegranate juice
1 tablespoon agave syrup
Fresh mint leaves for garnish

1 In a blender, combine blackberries, pomegranate juice, and agave syrup. Blend until smooth.

2 Strain the mixture into glasses.

3 Garnish with fresh mint leaves. Enjoy this harmonious blend of tartness and sweetness.

MINTY BERRY SPARKLE

A delightful beverage for a garden party or a brunch gathering, Minty Berry Sparkle combines the sweetness of berries with the freshness of mint, creating a cool and invigorating drink.

INGREDIENTS

1/2 cup mixed berries (strawberries, blueberries, raspberries)
1/4 cup fresh mint leaves
1 tablespoon agave syrup
Sparkling water
Crushed ice

1 Muddle mixed berries and mint leaves with agave syrup in a shaker.

2 Strain the mixture into two glasses filled with crushed ice. Top up with sparkling water. Gently stir.

3 Garnish with a mint sprig. Enjoy the refreshing Minty Berry Sparkle.

SUNSET BERRY SERENADE

Celebrate the beauty of a setting sun with the Sunset Berry Serenade, a visually stunning mocktail that's perfect for a romantic evening or a gathering with friends.

INGREDIENTS

I cup mixed berries (strawberries, blackberries, blueberries)
1/2 cup orange juice
I tablespoon agave syrup
Crushed ice

1 Combine mixed berries, orange juice, and agave syrup in a blender. Blend until smooth.

2 Fill glasses with crushed ice and pour the mixture over it.

3 Enjoy this refreshing vibrant mocktail.

ZEN BERRY REFRESHER

Achieve a sense of calm and rejuvenation with the Zen Berry Refresher, an invigorating drink that's perfect for a midday break or a post-workout cooldown.

INGREDIENTS

1/2 cup blueberries
1/2 cup cucumber slices
1 tablespoon mint leaves
1 tablespoon lime juice
Club soda

1 Muddle blueberries, cucumber slices, mint leaves, and lime juice in a shaker.

2 Strain the mixture into glasses and top with club soda.

3 Garnish with a cucumber wheel. Enjoy this cool flavorful instant relaxation.

BERRY BREEZE SPARKLER

Whether you're by the pool or dreaming of a beach vacation, the Berry Breeze Sparkler transports you to a tropical paradise, making it the perfect escape in a glass.

INGREDIENTS

1/2 cup raspberries
1/2 cup coconut water
1 tablespoon agave syrup
Sparkling water

1 Blend raspberries, coconut water, and agave syrup until smooth.

2 Strain into glasses and top with sparkling water.

3 Garnish with a raspberry on the rim. Enjoy this mocktail that's both sweet and hydrating.

BERRY BASIL BLISS

Elevate your brunch experience with the Berry Basil Bliss, a sophisticated and flavorful mocktail that complements a variety of breakfast dishes.

INGREDIENTS

I cup mixed berries (strawberries, blueberries, blackberries)
1/4 cup fresh basil leaves
I tablespoon honey
Lemonade

1 Muddle mixed berries, fresh basil leaves, and honey in a shaker.

2 Strain into glasses and top with lemonade.

3 Garnish with a basil sprig. A delightful mix of sweet berries and aromatic basil.

BERRY LEMONADE FIZZ

Sip on the Berry Basil Lemonade Fizz on a warm afternoon to experience a delightful combination of citrusy zing and herbal freshness.

INGREDIENTS

1/2 cup blueberries
1/2 cup fresh basil leaves
2 tablespoons agave syrup
Sparkling lemonade

1 Muddle blueberries, fresh basil leaves, and agave syrup in a shaker.

2 Strain into glasses and top with sparkling lemonade.

3 Enjoy and sip this zesty and herbaceous lemonade fizz.

TRIPLE BERRY CRUSH

Beat the heat with the Triple Berry Crush, a burst of fruity goodness that's perfect for a summer cooldown or a lively outdoor gathering.

INGREDIENTS

1/2 cup strawberries
1/2 cup blackberries
1/2 cup cranberry juice
I tablespoon maple syrup
Crushed ice
Sparkling water

1 Blend strawberries, blackberries, cranberry juice, and maple syrup until smooth.

2 Pour over crushed ice in glasses. Top with sparkling water.

3 Serve and enjoy this tangy and vibrant crush that awakens your taste buds.

POMEGRANATE ROSE SPARKLER

A delightful drink for a celebration or a romantic evening, the Pomegranate Rose Sparkler offers a unique blend of flavors with a touch of elegance.

INGREDIENTS

1/2 cup pomegranate juice
1 tablespoon rose water
1 tablespoon agave syrup
Sparkling water
Pomegranate arils for garnish
Ice cubes

1 Combine pomegranate juice, rose water, and agave syrup in a shaker.

2 Shake well and strain into two glasses filled with ice. Top up with plain sparkling water. Stir gently.

3 Garnish with pomegranate arils. Enjoy the exotic and floral Pomegranate Rose Sparkler.

RASPBERRY ROSE REFRESHER

Indulge in the Raspberry Rose Refresher for a touch of sophistication, making it an ideal choice for a bridal shower or a special celebration.

INGREDIENTS
1/2 cup raspberries
1/2 teaspoon rose water
1 tablespoon honey
Club soda

1 Muddle raspberries, rose water, and honey in a shaker.

2 Strain into glasses and top with club soda.

3 Garnish with a rose petal. Enjoy this elegant and fragrant refresher.

BERRY APPLE SPARKLE

Add a touch of excitement to your brunch with the Berry Apple Sparkle, a lively and effervescent mocktail that pairs well with a variety of dishes.

INGREDIENTS

1/2 cup mixed berries (strawberries, blueberries, blackberries)
1/4 cup fresh basil leaves
1 tablespoon agave syrup
1 cup apple juice
Sparkling water

1 Muddle mixed berries, fresh basil leaves, agave syrup, and apple juice in a shaker.

2 Strain into glasses and top with sparkling water.

3 Serve and enjoy this vibrant and bubbly concoction.

NUTTY CHERRY FIZZ

A delightful treat for a dessert-themed gathering or a romantic date night, the Nutty Cherry Fizz combines the richness of almonds with the sweetness of cherries.

INGREDIENTS

1/2 cup cherry juice
1/4 teaspoon almond extract
1 tablespoon agave syrup
Sparkling water
Maraschino cherries for garnish
Ice cubes

1 In a shaker, combine cherry juice, almond extract, and agave syrup.

2 Shake well and strain into two glasses filled with ice. Top up with sparkling water. Stir gently.

3 Top with maraschino cherries. Enjoy the sweet and nutty Cherry Almond Fizz.

RASPBERRY ROSE REFINEMENT

An exquisite choice for a sophisticated gathering or a special celebration, Raspberry Rose Refinement combines the tartness of raspberries with the floral elegance of rose water, creating a beautifully refined and luxurious mocktail experience.

INGREDIENTS

1/2 cup raspberry puree
1/4 teaspoon rose water
1 tablespoon honey
Sparkling water
Fresh raspberries for garnish
Ice cubes

1 In a shaker, combine raspberry puree, rose water, and honey. Shake well to blend the flavors, then strain into two glasses filled with ice.

2 Top up with sparkling water for an elegant effervescence.
Stir gently, allowing the Raspberry Rose Refinement to come to life.

3 Garnish with fresh raspberries for a visually appealing touch.

MINTY BERRY BREEZE

As summer approaches, the combination of sweet berries and cool mint provides a rejuvenating respite, making this mocktail perfect for picnics and outdoor gatherings.

INGREDIENTS

I cup mixed berries (strawberries, blueberries, raspberries)
1/4 cup fresh mint leaves
I tablespoon honey
Sparkling water
Ice cubes

1 Muddle berries, mint, and honey in a shaker.

2 Strain into glasses over ice. Top with sparkling water and stir gently.

3 Garnish with a mint sprig for a delightful burst of flavors.

STRAWBERRY BASIL FUSION

A perfect choice for a dinner party or a special occasion, the Strawberry Basil Fusion offers a complex flavor profile with the combination of sweet strawberries and savory basil.

INGREDIENTS

1/2 cup strawberry puree
1/4 cup fresh basil leaves
I tablespoon balsamic glaze
Sparkling water
Fresh strawberries for garnish
Ice cubes

1 In a shaker, mix strawberry puree, fresh basil leaves, and balsamic glaze.

2 Strain into two glasses filled with ice. Top up with sparkling water. Stir gently.

3 Garnish with fresh strawberries. Enjoy the unique and sophisticated Strawberry Basil Fusion.

APPLE ROSE ROMANCE

A charming blend of sweet apple and floral rose, the Apple Rose Romance is perfect for romantic evenings or special occasions. Sip and savor the enchanting experience, adding an elegant touch to your moments.

INGREDIENTS

1 cup apple juice
Rose water
Edible rose petals
Ginger ale

1 Mix apple juice with a dash of rose water.

2 Shake with ice, and strain into serving glasses.

3 Top with ginger ale and garnish with edible rose petals.

BLACKBERRY SAGE ELIXIR

A sophisticated choice for a cocktail-inspired mocktail, the Blackberry Sage Elixir is perfect for a dinner gathering or a celebration where you want to impress with a unique flavor combination.

INGREDIENTS

1/2 cup blackberry puree
1 tablespoon fresh sage leaves
1 tablespoon honey
Sparkling water
Blackberries for garnish
Ice cubes

1 In a shaker, muddle blackberry puree, fresh sage leaves, and honey.

2 Strain into two glasses filled with ice. Top up with sparkling water. Stir gently.

3 Garnish with blackberries. Sip and savor the earthy and herbal notes of the Blackberry Sage Elixir.

CITRUS BERRY FUSION

Kickstart your day with the Citrus Berry Fusion, a vitamin-packed mocktail that provides a burst of energy, perfect for a morning pick-me-up.

INGREDIENTS

1/2 cup mixed berries (blueberries, raspberries, strawberries)
1/2 cup orange juice
1 tablespoon honey
1/2 cup grapefruit soda

1 Blend mixed berries, orange juice, and honey until smooth.

2 Strain into glasses and top with grapefruit soda.

3 Serve and enjoy this citrusy explosion with a berry twist.

BLUEBERRY COCONUT BREEZE

Transport yourself to a tropical paradise with the Blueberry Basil Breeze, an exotic and refreshing mocktail perfect for a beach-themed party.

INGREDIENTS

I cup blueberries
1/4 cup fresh basil leaves
I tablespoon agave syrup
I cup coconut water

1 Muddle blueberries, fresh basil leaves, agave syrup, and coconut water in a shaker.

2 Strain into glasses.

3 Enjoy this tropical breeze with a hint of herbal sophistication.

BLUEBERRY BASIL BUBBLY

Celebrate the arrival of blueberry season with this vibrant mocktail, combining the sweetness of blueberries with the aromatic notes of fresh basil.

INGREDIENTS

1/2 cup blueberries
1/4 cup fresh basil leaves
1 tablespoon honey
Sparkling water
Ice cubes

1 Muddle blueberries, basil, and honey in a shaker.

2 Strain into glasses over ice. Top with sparkling water and stir gently.

3 Garnish with a basil leaf for a burst of fruity and herbal goodness.

CRANBERRY SPRITZER

Embrace the holiday spirit with the tartness of cranberry and the earthy aroma of sage. This mocktail is perfect for festive gatherings and cozy evenings by the fire.

INGREDIENTS

1/2 cup cranberry juice
I sprig of fresh sage
I tablespoon honey
Seltzer water
Crushed ice

1 Muddle fresh sage with honey in a shaker. Add cranberry juice and shake.

2 Strain into two glasses with crushed ice. Top with seltzer water.

3 Stir gently, and garnish with a sage leaf. Sip and savor the festive flavors.

QUADRUPLE BERRY DELIGHT

Celebrate the beauty of simplicity with the Quadruple Berry Delight, a classic and refreshing choice for any casual gathering or a quiet evening at home.

INGREDIENTS

1/2 cup strawberries
1/4 cup blueberries
1/4 cup blackberries
1 tablespoon agave syrup
1/2 cup cranberry juice

1 Blend strawberries, blueberries, blackberries, agave syrup, and cranberry juice until smooth.

2 Pour into glasses.

3 Serve and enjoy this delightful berries mocktail in every sip. Garnish with a berry spear if desired.

CHERRY ALMOND SPARKLE

This mocktail, with its rich cherry flavor and subtle almond undertones, is a festive choice for celebrating special occasions or ringing in the new year.

INGREDIENTS

1/2 cup cherry juice
1/4 teaspoon almond extract
1 tablespoon agave syrup
Sparkling water
Ice cubes

1 Mix cherry juice, almond extract, and agave syrup in a shaker.

2 Pour over ice and top with sparkling water. Stir gently.

3 Garnish with a cherry. Sip and experience the delightful pairing of cherry and almond.

BERRY GINGER SPLASH

Elevate your summer soiree with the Berry Basil Lemon Splash, a vibrant and effervescent mocktail that impresses with its unique combination of flavors.

INGREDIENTS

1/2 cup mixed berries (strawberries, raspberries, blackberries)
1/4 cup fresh basil leaves
I tablespoon honey
1/2 cup lemonade
1/2 cup ginger ale

1 Muddle mixed berries, fresh basil leaves, and honey in a shaker.

2 Strain into glasses and add lemonade and ginger ale.

3 Enjoy this citrusy splash with a hint of herbal sophistication.

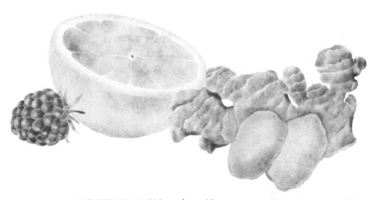

BLUEBERRY LAVENDER ELEGANCE

An excellent choice for a more upscale event or a romantic dinner, the Blueberry Lavender Elegance combines floral notes with the sweetness of blueberries for a truly refined experience.

INGREDIENTS

1/2 cup blueberries
1/4 teaspoon dried lavender buds
1 tablespoon honey
1 tablespoon lemon juice
Sparkling water
Ice cubes

1 In a shaker, muddle blueberries and dried lavender with honey and lemon juice.

2 Strain into two glasses filled with ice.

3 Top up with sparkling water, stir gently, and enjoy the sophisticated and aromatic Blueberry Lavender Elegance.

BERRY MINTY MELODY

Cool down on a hot day with the Berry Minty Melody, a light and invigorating mocktail that's perfect for a backyard barbecue or a lazy afternoon by the pool.

INGREDIENTS

1/2 cup mixed berries (blueberries, strawberries, raspberries)
1/4 cup mint leaves
1 tablespoon agave syrup
1 cup apple juice
Crushed ice

1 Muddle mixed berries, mint leaves, and agave syrup in a shaker.

2 Add apple juice and mix. Strain into glasses over crushed ice.

3 Enjoy this refreshing melody of berries and mint.

BERRY BASIL ELEGANCE

Elevate your beverage experience with the Berry Basil Elegance. A sophisticated refreshment, perfect for upscale events.

INGREDIENTS

1 cup mixed berries (strawberries, blueberries, raspberries)
1 tablespoon balsamic vinegar
Fresh basil leaves
Sparkling water

1 Muddle berries with balsamic vinegar and basil leaves.

2 Shake with ice and strain. Pour into serving glasses.

3 Top with sparkling water. Serve immediately and enjoy!

ISLAND
ENTERTAINING

PINEAPPLE COCONUT BLISS

Perfect for a hot summer day, the Pineapple Coconut Bliss provides a refreshing escape, combining tropical flavors with an artistic presentation.

INGREDIENTS

I cup pineapple juice
1/2 cup coconut water
2 tablespoons grenadine syrup
Ice cubes

1 Pour pineapple juice and coconut water over ice in a shaker. Shake well and strain into two glasses.

2 Slowly pour grenadine over the back of a spoon, letting it settle at the bottom.

3 Enjoy your stunning layered mocktail.

MANGO TANGO FIZZ

The Mango Tango Fizz is a vibrant and lively choice for a casual get-together, offering a perfect blend of sweetness and effervescence.

INGREDIENTS

1 cup mango juice
1/2 cup sparkling water
2 tablespoons lime juice
Fresh mint leaves

1 Mix mango juice and lime juice in a pitcher.

2 Divide the mixture between two glasses filled with ice.

3 Top each glass with sparkling water. Garnish with fresh mint leaves for a burst of aroma and flavor.

KIWI BASIL REFRESHER

Perfect for a summer picnic or a brunch gathering, the Kiwi Basil Refresher offers a unique blend of the tropical sweetness of kiwi with the aromatic freshness of basil, creating a refreshing and vibrant mocktail experience.

INGREDIENTS

2 ripe kiwis, peeled and sliced
1/4 cup fresh basil leaves
1 tablespoon honey
1 cup kiwi-strawberry flavored sparkling water
Kiwi slices and basil leaves for garnish
Ice cubes

1 In a blender, combine ripe kiwis, fresh basil leaves, and honey. Blend until smooth to create a flavorful kiwi-basil puree.

2 Strain the puree into two glasses filled with ice. Top up with kiwi-strawberry-flavored sparkling water.

3 Stir gently, garnish with kiwi slices and basil leaves. Sip and savor the delightful Kiwi Basil Refresher.

COCONUT MINT MOJITO

A delightful choice for a brunch gathering, the Coconut Mint Mojito combines the classic Mojito feel with a tropical coconut twist.

INGREDIENTS

1 cup coconut water
1/2 cup fresh lime juice
2 tablespoons mint leaves
Soda water
Sliced lime (for garnish)

1 Muddle mint leaves in a glass. Add coconut water and lime juice, stirring well.

2 Fill the glass with ice and top it off with soda water.

3 Garnish with sliced lime for a zesty finish.

LYCHEE LAVENDER FUSION

Ideal for a sophisticated gathering or a special occasion, Lychee Lavender Fusion combines sweet and exotic lychee with the aromatic and floral notes of lavender, creating a uniquely refreshing and refined mocktail experience.

INGREDIENTS

1 1/2 cup lychee juice
1/4 teaspoon dried lavender buds
1 tablespoon honey
1 cup lavender-infused water*
Lychee fruits for garnish
Ice cubes

*page 120

1 In a shaker, combine lychee juice, dried lavender buds, and honey. Shake well to infuse the flavors, then strain into two glasses filled with ice.

2 Top up with lavender-infused water for a floral effervescence. Stir gently to blend the unique fusion of lychee and lavender.

3 Garnish with fresh lychee fruits for an elegant touch.

PASSIONFRUIT PARADISE PUNCH

Transport yourself to an exotic destination
with the Passionfruit Paradise Punch,
a sweet and tangy treat perfect for a
weekend escape.

INGREDIENTS

1/2 cup passionfruit juice
1/2 cup orange juice
2 tablespoons agave syrup
Coconut water
Pineapple slices (for garnish)

1 Mix passionfruit juice, orange juice, and agave syrup in a pitcher.

2 Pour over ice in two glasses. Top with coconut water.

3 Garnish with pineapple slices for a taste of the tropics.

PINEAPPLE BASIL FRESHNESS

This mocktail is perfect for a garden party, offering a unique blend of tropical sweetness and herbal freshness.

INGREDIENTS

I cup fresh pineapple chunks
1/4 cup fresh basil leaves
I tablespoon agave syrup
Crushed ice

1 Blend pineapple chunks, basil leaves, and agave syrup until smooth.

2 Strain the mixture into two glasses filled with crushed ice.
Add sparkling water.

3 Garnish with a basil sprig for a delightful herbal twist.

VELVET SUNSET BLISS

This vibrant mocktail offers a refreshing tropical flavor, perfect for beach-themed events.

INGREDIENTS

I cup pomegranate juice
1/2 cup coconut water
I tablespoon agave syrup
Ice cubes

1 In a shaker, combine pomegranate juice, coconut water, and agave syrup.

2 Shake well and strain into two glasses filled with ice.

3 Serve and enjoy immediately!

GUAVA ORANGE SPARKLER

Enhance your brunch experience with the Guava Sparkler, a visually appealing and refreshing option that combines tropical and citrus flavors.

INGREDIENTS

1/2 cup guava juice
1/2 cup orange juice
1/4 cup pomegranate juice
Sparkling water

1 Mix guava juice and orange juice in a pitcher.

2 Pour over ice into two glasses. Slowly add pomegranate juice, letting it settle at the bottom.

3 Top with sparkling water for a bubbly finish. Enjoy immediately!

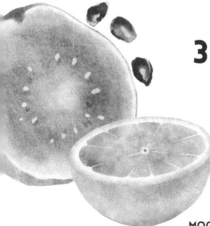

WATERMELON MINT REFRESHER

Stay cool on a hot day with the Watermelon Mint Refresher, a hydrating and invigorating mocktail that screams summer.

INGREDIENTS

1 cup fresh watermelon chunks
1/4 cup fresh lime juice
2 tablespoons mint leaves
Crushed ice

1 Blend watermelon chunks, lime juice, and mint leaves until smooth.

2 Strain into two glasses filled with crushed ice.

3 Serve and enjoy the perfect balance of sweet and minty freshness.

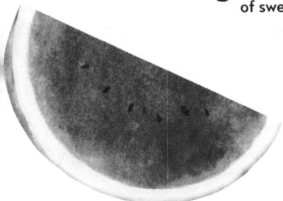

BEACHSIDE SERENITY SPLASH

Ideal for a summer luau or a beach-themed gathering, the Beachside Serenity Splash brings together tropical flavors, providing a taste of the islands in every sip.

INGREDIENTS

1/2 cup pineapple juice
1/4 cup coconut milk
1/4 cup mango puree
1 tablespoon agave syrup
Club soda
Pineapple wedge for garnish

1 In a blender, combine pineapple juice, coconut milk, mango puree, and agave syrup. Blend until smooth.

2 Divide the mixture into two glasses filled with ice. Top up with club soda. Stir gently.

3 Garnish with a pineapple wedge. Sip and transport yourself to a Tropical Paradise.

TROPICAL HIBISCUS HUES

Embrace the calming vibes of a tropical evening with the Tropical Hibiscus Hues, a delightful mocktail with a touch of floral elegance.

INGREDIENTS

1 cup hibiscus tea (cooled)
1 cup pineapple juice
1 tablespoon agave syrup
Ice cubes

1 Mix cooled hibiscus tea, pineapple juice, and agave syrup in a shaker.

2 Strain into two glasses over ice.

3 Serve and enjoy this vibrant and floral drink that's both refreshing and soothing.

KIWI CITRUS ZING

Kickstart your day with the Kiwi Citrus Zing, a vitamin-packed mocktail that brings a burst of energy and a hint of tropical flair.

INGREDIENTS

3 ripe kiwis
I cup orange juice
1/4 cup lime juice
Agave syrup (to taste)

1 Peel and dice kiwis. Blend diced kiwis, orange juice, lime juice, and agave syrup until smooth.

2 Strain into two glasses over ice.

3 Enjoy this tangy and invigorating drink with a burst of kiwi freshness.

HIBISCUS GINGER FIZZ

As spring unfolds, the vibrant colors of hibiscus and the warmth of ginger come together in this mocktail, providing a delightful and invigorating beverage for any occasion.

INGREDIENTS

1/2 cup hibiscus tea (cooled)
1/2 teaspoon freshly grated ginger
1 tablespoon honey
Sparkling water
Ice cubes

1 Mix hibiscus tea, grated ginger, and honey in a shaker.

2 Pour over ice and top with sparkling water. Stir gently.

3 Garnish with a hibiscus flower. Sip and enjoy the floral and spicy fusion.

BLUE LAGOON ELIXIR

Unwind by the pool or at a summer picnic with the Blue Lagoon Elixir, a striking and flavorful mocktail that stands out in any setting.

INGREDIENTS

I cup blueberry juice
1/2 cup coconut milk
I tablespoon agave syrup
Ice cubes

1 Combine blueberry juice, coconut milk, and agave syrup in a shaker.

2 Shake well and strain into two glasses over ice.

3 Enjoy the vibrant blue color and unique flavor of this stunning and delicious drink.

TROPICAL PARADISE REFRESHER

With its exotic blend, this mocktail transports you to an island retreat, making it an ideal choice for lounging by the pool or enjoying on a staycation.

INGREDIENTS

1/2 cup coconut water
1/2 cup pineapple juice
1/4 cup mango puree
1 tablespoon lime juice
Ice cubes

1 Combine coconut water, pineapple juice, mango puree, and lime juice in a shaker.

2 Shake well and pour over ice in serving glasses.

3 Garnish with a lime wheel. Sip and be transported to a tropical haven.

WATERMELON ROSE QUENCHER

Ideal for a summer afternoon or a refreshing treat after exercise, this mocktail combines the hydrating properties of watermelon with the floral elegance of rose water, offering a cooling and invigorating experience.

INGREDIENTS

2 cups fresh watermelon chunks
I tablespoon rose water
I tablespoon agave syrup
I cup coconut water
Fresh mint leaves for garnish
Ice cubes

1 In a blender, puree fresh watermelon chunks until smooth. Strain the watermelon puree into two glasses filled with ice. Add rose water and agave syrup for a floral and sweet twist.

2 Top up with refreshing coconut water. Stir gently, ensuring the flavors blend harmoniously.

3 Garnish with fresh mint leaves for an extra burst of freshness.

DRAGONFRUIT DREAM SIPPER

Embark on a flavor adventure with the
Dragonfruit Dream Sipper, a tropical mocktail
that captivates both, the taste buds,
and the eyes.

INGREDIENTS

1/2 cup dragon fruit
puree
1/2 cup coconut water
1 tablespoon honey
Fresh mint leaves (for
garnish)

1 Blend dragon fruit puree, coconut water, and honey until smooth.

2 Strain into two glasses over ice.

3 Garnish with fresh mint leaves for a visually stunning and refreshing drink.

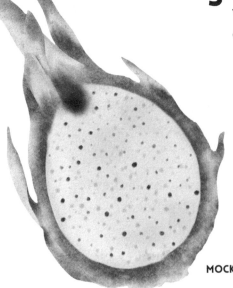

PAPAYA PASSION FUSION

Indulge in the Papaya Passion Fusion as a dessert companion or a post-dinner treat, savoring the tropical richness of papaya and passionfruit.

INGREDIENTS

I cup fresh papaya chunks
1/2 cup passionfruit juice
I tablespoon honey
Ice cubes

1 Blend fresh papaya chunks, passionfruit juice, and honey until smooth.

2 Strain into two glasses over ice.

3 Enjoy this luscious and exotic blend that captivates the taste buds.

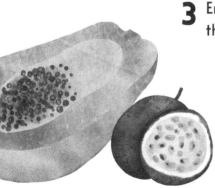

COCONUT MANGO DELIGHT

Unwind after a hectic day with the Minty Mango Delight, a soothing mocktail that combines the tropical sweetness of mango with a hint of refreshing mint.

INGREDIENTS

I cup mango juice
1/2 cup coconut water
2 tablespoons fresh lime juice
Fresh mint leaves (for garnish)

1 Combine mango juice, coconut water, and fresh lime juice in a shaker.

2 Shake well and strain into two glasses over ice.

3 Garnish with fresh mint leaves for a cooling and tropical treat.

LYCHEE LIME FUSION

Elevate your mocktail experience with the Lychee Lime Fusion, a refreshing blend that balances the sweetness of lychee with the tartness of lime.

INGREDIENTS

1/2 cup lychee juice
1/2 cup fresh lime juice
1 tablespoon simple syrup*
Lychee fruit (for garnish)

*page 119

1 Combine lychee juice, fresh lime juice, and simple syrup in a shaker.

2 Strain into two glasses over ice.

3 Garnish with lychee fruit for a sweet and citrusy delight.

MANGO MINT MOJITO

Whether you're dreaming of a beach vacation or simply looking for a refreshing escape, this mango mint mojito brings a taste of the tropics to your glass.

INGREDIENTS

1 cup mango chunks
1/4 cup fresh mint leaves
1 tablespoon agave syrup
1 tablespoon lime juice
Club soda
Ice cubes

1 Muddle mango, mint, agave syrup, and lime juice in a glass.

2 Add ice and top with club soda. Stir gently.

3 Garnish with a mint sprig. Enjoy the tropical twist of mango and mint.

COCONUT KIWI CRUSH

Stay cool and refreshed with the Coconut Kiwi Crush, a delightful mocktail that brings together the creaminess of coconut and the tanginess of kiwi.

INGREDIENTS

1 cup coconut water
1/2 cup kiwi juice
1 tablespoon agave syrup
Crushed ice

1 Combine coconut water, kiwi juice, and agave syrup in a blender.

2 Strain into two glasses filled with crushed ice.

3 Serve and enjoy the Coconut Kiwi Crush delivers a tropical burst with a coconut twist.

PINEAPPLE MINT SPLASH

Refreshing and invigorating, it combines tropical sweetness with a cool burst of mint. Perfect for warm days or casual gatherings, it offers a revitalizing experience with every sip for those seeking a light and uplifting beverage.

INGREDIENTS

I cup pineapple juice
Fresh mint leaves
I tablespoon agave syrup
Sparkling water

1 Muddle fresh mint leaves with pineapple juice and agave syrup.

2 Shake with ice, and strain into serving glasses.

3 Finish with sparkling water. Enjoy immediately!

SPICY
SOIREE

ROSEMARY GRAPEFRUIT FIZZ

With the arrival of winter, the aromatic combination of rosemary and grapefruit offers a crisp and invigorating experience, making it an excellent choice for festive gatherings.

INGREDIENTS

1 cup grapefruit juice
1 sprig fresh rosemary
1 tablespoon agave syrup
Soda water
Ice cubes

1 Muddle fresh rosemary with agave syrup in a shaker. Add grapefruit juice and ice.

2 Shake, and then strain the mixture into two glasses. Top with soda water. Stir gently.

3 Garnish with a rosemary sprig. Revel in the herbal and citrus fusion.

MELON MINT SERENITY

Perfect for a spa day or a relaxing evening on the patio, Melon Mint Serenity provides a calming and refreshing experience with the combination of melon and mint.

INGREDIENTS

1/2 cup honeydew melon, cubed
1/4 cup fresh mint leaves
1 tablespoon lime juice
1 tablespoon agave syrup
Sparkling water
Mint sprigs for garnish
Ice cubes

1 In a blender, combine honeydew melon, mint leaves, lime juice, and agave syrup. Blend until smooth.

2 Divide the mixture into two glasses filled with ice. Top up with sparkling water. Stir gently.

3 Garnish with mint sprigs. Enjoy the refreshing Melon Mint Serenity.

MANGO CHILI FIESTA

Spice up your festivities with this bold mocktail. It combines sweet mango with a hint of chili for a unique experience. Perfect for parties or those seeking a tropical drink with a spicy kick. Get ready to add a flavorful twist to your celebration!

INGREDIENTS

I cup mango puree
1/4 teaspoon chili powder
Lime wedges
Club soda

1 Mix mango puree with chili powder.

2 Shake with ice, and strain into serving glasses.

3 Serve with a squeeze of lime and top with club soda.

VANILLA PEAR FIZZ

With winter approaching, the comforting blend of vanilla and pear in this mocktail provides a warm and soothing beverage, perfect for holiday celebrations.

INGREDIENTS

1 cup pear juice
1/2 teaspoon vanilla extract
1 tablespoon maple syrup
Ginger ale
Ice cubes

1 Mix pear juice, vanilla extract, and maple syrup in a shaker.

2 Pour over ice and top with ginger ale. Stir gently.

3 Garnish with a pear slice. Enjoy the sweet and aromatic notes of vanilla and pear.

CUCUMBER SAGE SERENITY

Crafted for tranquility, this drink is perfect for spa days or quiet evenings. It provides a calming experience, making it an ideal choice for moments of relaxation and contemplation.

INGREDIENTS

I cup cucumber juice
I tablespoon honey
Fresh sage leaves
Tonic water

1 Combine cucumber juice, honey, and sage leaves.

2 Shake with ice and strain. Pour into serving glasses. Top with tonic water for a calming mocktail.

3 Sip and immerse yourself in this uniquely crafted blend for a serene escape.

CARDAMOM APPLE SPARKLER

Embrace the fall season with the Cardamom Apple Sparkler, a warm and spiced mocktail that combines the comforting flavors of apple and cranberry with a hint of cardamom.

INGREDIENTS

3 cardamom pods, crushed
1/2 cup apple cider
1/4 cup cranberry juice
1 tablespoon maple syrup
Club soda

1 Infuse crushed cardamom pods in apple cider

2 Mix with cranberry juice and maple syrup.

3 Top with club soda and stir gently. Enjoy your cozy drink.

POMEGRANATE MINT FIZZ

Celebrate the transition from winter to spring with the vibrant colors of pomegranate. This mocktail offers a delightful mix of sweetness and effervescence.

INGREDIENTS

1/2 cup pomegranate juice
1/4 cup fresh mint leaves
1 tablespoon simple syrup*
Club soda
Ice cubes

*page 119

1 In a glass, muddle mint leaves with simple syrup. Add ice, pour pomegranate juice, and top with club soda.

2 Shake with ice and strain. Pour into the serving glasses.

3 Garnish with pomegranate arils for a burst of flavor.

PEPPERMINT BERRY BREEZE

Elevate a holiday celebration with the Peppermint Berry Breeze, a festive and minty mocktail that combines the freshness of peppermint with the sweetness of mixed berries.

INGREDIENTS

10 fresh peppermint leaves
1/2 cup mixed berries (strawberries, blueberries, raspberries)
1/4 cup lime juice
1 tablespoon honey
Sparkling water

1 Muddle peppermint with mixed berries, lime juice, and honey. Shake with ice.

2 Strain into glasses. Add more ice if desired.

3 Top with sparkling water. Serve immediately and enjoy!

SAFFRON CITRUS ELEGANCE

Indulge in sophistication with the Saffron Citrus Elegance, a luxurious mocktail that combines the exotic essence of saffron with the citrusy notes of orange and grapefruit. Perfect for a dinner party or special occasion.

INGREDIENTS

A pinch of saffron threads
1/2 cup orange juice
1/4 cup grapefruit juice
1 tablespoon agave syrup
Soda water

1 Steep saffron threads in hot water and mix with orange and grapefruit juices, and agave syrup.

2 Allow to chill. Add ice to glasses. Pour mocktail over ice.

3 Top with soda water. Enjoy immediately.

CRANBERRY SAGE SPARKLE

Perfect for a festive occasion or a holiday gathering, the Cranberry Sage Sparkle combines the tartness of cranberries with the earthy essence of sage, creating a refreshing and festive mocktail experience.

INGREDIENTS

1/2 cup cranberry juice
1/4 cup sage-infused simple syrup*
1 tablespoon fresh lime juice
Club soda
Fresh cranberries for garnish
Ice cubes

*page 119

1 In a shaker, mix cranberry juice, sage-infused simple syrup, and fresh lime juice. Strain the flavorful mixture into two glasses filled with ice.

2 Top up with club soda for a sparkling twist. Stir gently to blend the flavors and garnish with fresh cranberries.

3 Enjoy the vibrant herbal notes of the Cranberry Sage Sparkle.

GINGER PEACH ZING

Perfect for a barbecue or a casual get-together, the Ginger Peach Zing offers a spicy kick from ginger combined with the sweetness of ripe peaches.

INGREDIENTS

1/2 cup peach nectar
1 tablespoon fresh ginger, grated
1 tablespoon honey
1 cup ginger ale
Peach slices for garnish
Ice cubes

1 In a shaker, combine peach nectar, grated ginger, and honey.

2 Shake well and strain into two glasses filled with ice. Top up with ginger ale, and stir gently.

3 Garnish with peach slices. Enjoy the zesty and invigorating Ginger Peach Zing.

CUCUMBER BASIL BREEZE

Perfect for a light and healthy alternative, the Cucumber Basil Breeze is great for post-workout refreshment or as a hydrating drink during a spa day.

INGREDIENTS
1/2 cucumber, sliced
1/4 cup fresh basil leaves
1 tablespoon simple syrup*
1 tablespoon lime juice
Sparkling water
Ice cubes

*page 119

1 In a shaker, muddle cucumber slices and basil leaves with simple syrup and lime juice.

2 Strain into two glasses filled with ice. Top up with sparkling water. Stir gently.

3 Garnish with a cucumber wheel. Enjoy the crisp and cooling Cucumber Basil Breeze.

OREGANO BERRY BREEZE

Enhance a summer barbecue with the Oregano Berry Breeze, a vibrant combination of oregano, mixed berries, and citrusy orange juice.

INGREDIENTS

1 tablespoon fresh oregano leaves
1/2 cup mixed berries (blackberries, raspberries, blueberries)
1/2 cup orange juice
1 tablespoon honey
Club soda

1 Muddle oregano with mixed berries and honey. Add orange juice. Shake with ice.

2 Add ice to glasses. Strain the drink into two glasses.

3 Top with club soda. Serve immediately and sip.

MINTY MELON SPARKLE

Ideal for a post-workout refreshment, the Minty Melon Sparkle combines hydrating watermelon, zesty lime, and invigorating mint, creating a revitalizing drink.

INGREDIENTS

1 cup watermelon chunks
8 fresh mint leaves
1 tablespoon lime juice
Ginger ale
Ice cubes

1 Blend watermelon, mint, and lime juice.

2 Strain into glasses with ice, top with ginger ale, and stir gently.

3 Garnish with a mint sprig. Serve immediately and enjoy your refreshing mocktail.

ROSEMARY CITRUS ZING

Perfect for a dinner gathering, the Rosemary Citrus Zing mocktail offers a sophisticated blend of herbal rosemary, tangy citrus, and a hint of sweetness, creating a classy and unique mocktail.

INGREDIENTS

2 sprigs fresh rosemary
1/2 cup orange juice
1/4 cup cranberry juice
1 tablespoon agave syrup
Soda water

1 Infuse rosemary in orange and cranberry juices. Add agave syrup and shake with ice.

2 Strain into glasses. Add extra ice to your serving glasses

3 Top with soda water, serve immediately and enjoy!

CUCUMBER BASIL BLISS

As spring blossoms, the crispness of cucumber and the herbal touch of basil provide a light and invigorating beverage, perfect for garden gatherings.

INGREDIENTS

1 cup cucumber slices
1/4 cup fresh basil leaves
1 tablespoon agave syrup
1 tablespoon lime juice
Tonic water
Ice cubes

1 Muddle cucumber, basil, agave syrup, and lime juice in a glass.

2 Add ice and top with tonic water and stir gently.

3 Garnish with a cucumber wheel. Enjoy the cool, herbal notes.

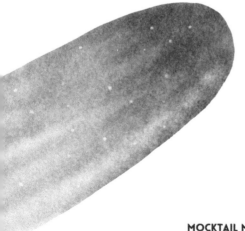

VANILLA PEACH DREAM

A comforting drink for a cozy night in or a dessert pairing, the Vanilla Peach Dream combines the warmth of vanilla with the sweetness of ripe peaches.

INGREDIENTS

1/2 cup peach nectar
1/4 teaspoon vanilla extract
1 tablespoon honey
Sparkling water
Peach slices for garnish
Ice cubes

1 In a shaker, combine peach nectar, vanilla extract, and honey.

2 Shake well and strain into two glasses filled with ice. Top up with vanilla-flavored sparkling water. Stir gently.

3 Garnish with peach slices. Indulge in the sweet and creamy Vanilla Peach Dream.

CARAMEL APPLE SPARKLER

Perfect for a fall gathering or a cozy night, this mocktail adds a sweet twist with caramel, combining the warmth of cinnamon and the sweetness of apples for a delightful and indulgent experience.

INGREDIENTS

1 cup apple juice
1/4 teaspoon ground cinnamon
2 tablespoons caramel syrup
Sparkling water
Apple slices for garnish
Ice cubes

1 In a shaker, combine apple juice, ground cinnamon, and caramel syrup for a sweet twist. Strain the flavorful mixture into two glasses filled with ice.

2 Top up with sparkling water. Stir gently to blend the flavors and garnish with apple slices.

3 Delight in the cozy and comforting experience of the Caramel Apple Cinnamon Sparkler.

PEACHES & TEA ZINGER

With the arrival of juicy peaches, this mocktail offers a balance of warmth and freshness, making it a delightful companion for a sunny afternoon on the porch.

INGREDIENTS

I cup peach nectar
1/2 teaspoon freshly grated ginger
I tablespoon honey
I cup iced tea
Ice cubes

1 Mix peach nectar, grated ginger, and honey in a shaker.

2 Pour over ice and top with iced tea.

3 Garnish with a peach slice. Sip to experience a harmonious blend of fruity sweetness with a ginger kick.

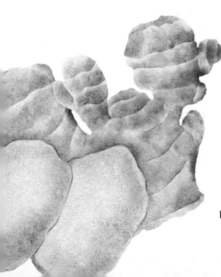

LAVENDER LEMON FIZZ

A delightful companion for a leisurely reading session, the Lavender Lemon Fizz combines the calming essence of lavender with the citrusy kick of lemonade.

INGREDIENTS

2 tablespoon lavender-infused water*
1/2 cup lemonade
1/4 cup elderflower syrup
Club soda
Lemon slices

*page 120

1 Mix with lavender-infused water with lemonade and elderflower syrup.

2 Pour the drink into your glasses over ice. Top with club soda.

3 Garnish with lemon slices. Sip and enjoy!

APPLE CINNAMON SPICE DELIGHT

Ideal for a fall gathering or a cozy night by the fireplace, this mocktail brings together the warmth of cinnamon and the sweetness of apples.

INGREDIENTS

I cup apple juice
1/4 teaspoon ground cinnamon
I tablespoon maple syrup
Sparkling water
Apple slices for garnish
Ice cubes

1 In a shaker, mix apple juice, ground cinnamon, and maple syrup.

2 Strain into two glasses filled with ice. Top up with cinnamon-flavored sparkling water. Stir gently.

3 Garnish with apple slices. Indulge in the cozy and comforting Apple Cinnamon Spice Delight.

PEACH BASIL EUPHORIA

Perfect for a summer celebration or a relaxing afternoon, the Peach Basil Euphoria combines the sweetness of ripe peaches with the aromatic essence of fresh basil, offering a euphoric and uplifting mocktail experience.

INGREDIENTS

6 ripe peaches, sliced
1/4 cup fresh basil leaves
I tablespoon honey
Sparkling water
Peach slices and basil sprigs for garnish
Ice cubes

1 In a shaker, muddle ripe peaches and fresh basil leaves with honey. Strain the muddled mixture into two glasses filled with ice.

2 Top up with peach-flavored sparkling water for effervescence. Stir gently, allowing the flavors to meld.

3 Garnish with peach slices and basil sprigs for an extra touch of freshness. Immerse yourself in the delightful Peach Basil Euphoria.

CHAMOMILE PEACH DREAM

Unwind after a hectic day with the Chamomile Peach Dream, a soothing blend of chamomile tea, sweet peach, and hydrating coconut water.

INGREDIENTS

2 chamomile tea bags
I cup peach nectar
1/2 cup coconut water
I tablespoon agave syrup
Crushed ice

1 Steep chamomile tea bags in hot water and mix with peach nectar, coconut water, and agave syrup.

2 Add crushed ice to your glasses. Chill your drink, then pour over crushed ice.

3 Enjoy immediately!

HIBISCUS GINGER FUSION

A perfect choice for a garden party or a summer soirée, the Hibiscus Ginger Fusion offers a delightful combination of floral and spicy notes.

INGREDIENTS

1/2 cup hibiscus tea, chilled
1/4 cup ginger simple syrup*
1 tablespoon lemon juice
Sparkling water
Hibiscus petals for garnish
Ice cubes

*page 119

1 In a shaker, combine chilled hibiscus tea, ginger syrup, and lemon juice.

2 Strain into two glasses filled with ice. Top up with sparkling water. Stir gently.

3 Garnish with hibiscus petals. Enjoy the unique and invigorating Hibiscus Ginger Fusion.

THYME BERRY FIZZ

Enjoy the Thyme Berry Fizz during brunch with friends, as it combines the earthiness of thyme with the vibrant burst of mixed berries for a delightful and socializing experience.

INGREDIENTS

5 sprigs fresh thyme
1/2 cup mixed berries
(strawberries,
blueberries,
raspberries)
1 tablespoon honey
Sparkling water
Ice cubes

1 Muddle thyme with mixed berries and honey.

2 Shake with ice, strain into glasses, and top with sparkling water.

3 Garnish with thyme sprigs. Serve immediately and enjoy!

CINNAMON APPLE SPARKLE

Welcome the holiday season with the Cinnamon Apple Sparkle, a warm and festive mocktail that combines the comforting aroma of cinnamon with the sweet and tart notes of apple and pomegranate.

INGREDIENTS

1 cinnamon stick
1/2 cup apple juice
1/4 cup pomegranate juice
1 tablespoon honey
Club soda

1 Infuse the apple juice with the cinnamon stick. Mix apple juice with pomegranate juice and honey.

2 Top with club soda and stir gently. Pour into your serving glasses.

3 Serve immediately and enjoy!

RECIPE RESOURCES

SIMPLE SYRUP

Simple syrup is just that - simple! Using this simple syrup recipe as a base and infusing it with various flavors can take your mocktail to the next level, with very little extra work.

INGREDIENTS

1 cup water
1 cup white sugar

1 Heat the water in a pot - do not boil. Add the sugar and stir to dissolve it completely.

2 Turn off the heat, and allow the syrup to cool completely. Store in a glass container in the refrigerator for up to three weeks.

VARIATIONS

MINT, ROSEMARY, SAGE, BASIL
After removing the syrup from the heat, add 1-2 cups of the preferred herb. Allow to steep for a minimum of one hour.

Strain out the herb and store it as directed.

GINGER
Grate 4 oz of fresh ginger, and place it in the water before heating. Make the syrup as directed.

After cooling completely, strain out the ginger and store it accordingly.

LAVENDER-INFUSED WATER

This simple addition will make your mocktails sing with the floral notes of lavender.

INGREDIENTS

2 cup water

2 teaspoons lavender buds

1 Bring the water to a boil in a pot. Prepare a glass jar by adding the lavender buds.

2 Carefully pour the boiling water into the jar. Allow to cool completely, then store in the refrigerator for 24 hours before using.

INDEX

INDEX

INDEX

Made in the USA
Coppell, TX
03 November 2024

39348220R00069